Blessed is the spot, and the house, and the place, and the city, and the heart, and the mountain,

A Conversation with GOD

and the refuge, and the cave, and the valley, and the land, and the sea, and the island, and the meadow where mention of God hath been made, and His praise glorified.

—Bahá'u'lláh

Declan was passing a group of grown-ups
when he heard them talking about
a conversation with God.

He knew when people have
a conversation they talk and
listen to each other but
he did not know how to have
a conversation with God.

Declan had often wanted to have a
conversation with God, but Declan felt God
must be far away.

He began to think about how to have
such a conversation.

He decided to try the toy telephone
his brother Matthew had made with their mom.

He talked and listened
and listened and talked

but did not hear anything...

The next day Declan's friends
were playing with walkie-talkies.

"Aha!" said Declan,
"maybe God has a walkie-talkie
and if I call Him we can have
a conversation."

9

But no matter how hard he tried
and how often he called, Declan never
managed to have that conversation
with God.

Declan decided to ask his cousin Haydar.

"Haydar, do you know how to have a
conversation with God?" asked Declan.
"I think He is very far away."

"Hmm..."

"I know!

When I want to talk to someone far away,

like Teta, I call her on"

"ZOOM!"

Declan and Haydar shouted together.

They ran to the computer but, look as they may,
they could not find God in the list of contacts.

"What about sending an email asking God to call?"
asked Haydar.

"Good idea!" agreed Declan.
"Hmm... I cannot find Him in the address book,"
Haydar said sadly.

"Let us try my daddy's phone.
He is always having conversations!"
Declan suggested.

But try as they may, they could not get
his daddy's phone to unlock.

"Oh my!
I do not think I will ever have a conversation
with God!" Declan said sadly.

The next day Declan was lying on a blanket in the backyard looking up at the clouds in the sky.

"Hello God," he shouted.

"Are you there?" he shouted even louder.

"It is me, Declan. I want to TALK WITH YOU!"

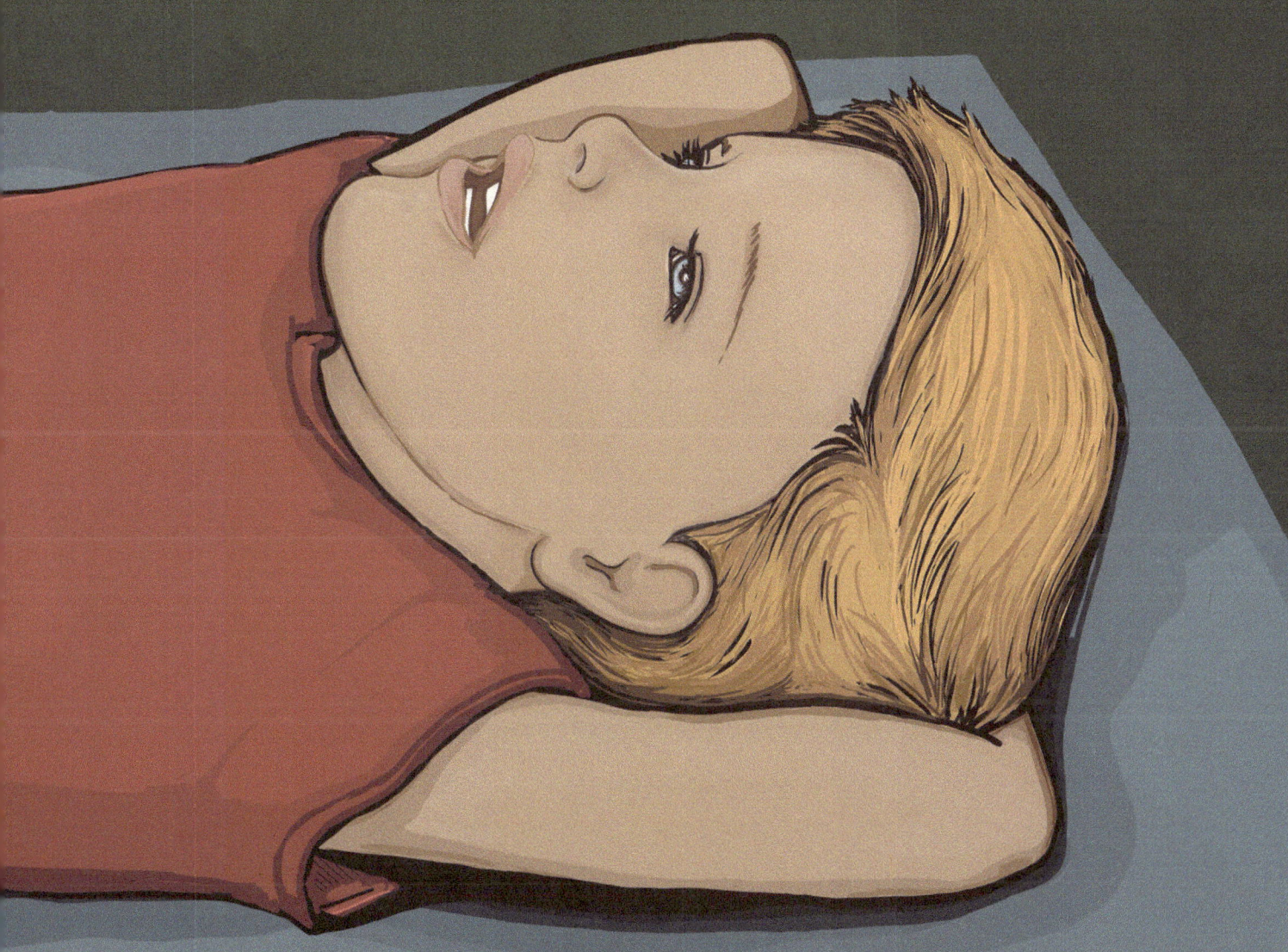

Declan's mom came running out.

"Are you okay Declan?" she asked.

"Yes,

I am trying to have a . . .

conversation with God."

explained Declan.

"Mommy, do you know how?"

Declan's mom smiled at him and hugged him tightly.

"Yes, Declan. Prayer is conversation with God." she explained.

"Prayer?" asked Declan.

"Prayer is conversation with God?"

"Yes, dear Declan."

Declan jumped up,
shouted "Of course!",
ran into the house,
dashed up the stairs,
burst into his bedroom,
leapt onto his bed,
picked up his prayer book,
sat upright,
took a deep breath,
closed his eyes,

and slowly,
oh so slowly,
Declan had a wonderful conversation with God.

Later, Declan's mom came into his room.

"Mom!
I had a wonderful
conversation
with God!"

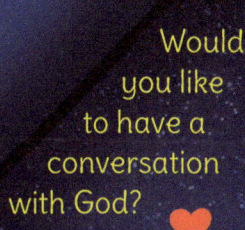

Would
you like
to have a
conversation
with God?

O God,
guide me,
protect me,
make of me a shining lamp
and a brilliant star.

Thou art the Mighty
and the Powerful.

—'Abdu'l-Bahá

O my Lord! O my Lord!

I am a child of tender years. Nourish me from

the breast of Thy mercy, train me in the bosom of

Thy love, educate me in the school of Thy guidance and

develop me under the shadow of Thy bounty. Deliver me

from darkness, make me a brilliant light; free me from

unhappiness, make me a flower of the rose garden; suffer

me to become a servant of Thy threshold and confer upon

me the disposition and nature of the righteous; make me

a cause of bounty to the human world, and crown my

head with the diadem of eternal life.

Verily, Thou art the Powerful, the Mighty,

the Seer, the Hearer.

—'Abdu'l-Bahá

Strive that your actions day by day may be beautiful prayers.

Turn towards God, and seek always to do that which is right and noble.
Enrich the poor, raise the fallen, comfort the sorrowful, bring healing
to the sick, reassure the fearful, rescue the oppressed, bring hope
to the hopeless, shelter the destitute!

—'Abdu'l-Bahá

I am, O my God, but a tiny seed which Thou hast sown in the soil of Thy love, and caused to spring forth by the hand of Thy bounty.

—Bahá'u'lláh

O Thou the Compassionate God. Bestow upon me a heart which, like unto a glass, may be illumined with the light of Thy love, and confer upon me thoughts which may change this world into a rose garden through the outpourings of heavenly grace.

—'Abdu'l-Bahá

O Lord! I am a child; enable me to grow beneath the shadow of Thy loving-kindness. I am a tender plant; cause me to be nurtured through the outpourings of the clouds of Thy bounty. I am a sapling of the garden of love; make me into a fruitful tree.
Thou art the Mighty and the Powerful, and Thou art the All-Loving, the All-Knowing, the All-Seeing.

—'Abdu'l-Bahá

Thy name is my healing, O my God,

and remembrance of Thee is my remedy.

Nearness to Thee is my hope, and love for Thee

is my companion. Thy mercy to me is my healing

and my succor in both this world and the world

to come. Thou, verily, art the All-Bountiful,

the All-Knowing, the All-Wise.

—Bahá'u'lláh

O God, my God,
my Beloved,
my heart's Desire.

—The Báb

Immerse yourselves
in the ocean of My words,
that ye may unravel its secrets,
and discover all the
pearls of wisdom that
lie hid in its depths.

—Bahá'u'lláh

O Thou kind Lord! These lovely children are the handiwork of the fingers of Thy might and the wondrous signs of Thy greatness. O God! Protect these children, graciously assist them to be educated and enable them to render service to the world of humanity. O God! These children are pearls, cause them to be nurtured within the shell of Thy loving-kindness.

Thou art the Bountiful, the All-Loving.

—'Abdu'l-Bahá

O God! Educate these children. These children are
the plants of Thine orchard, the flowers of Thy meadow,
the roses of Thy garden. Let Thy rain fall upon them; let the
Sun of Reality shine upon them with Thy love. Let Thy breeze
refresh them in order that they may be trained, grow and
develop, and appear in the utmost beauty.
Thou art the Giver. Thou art the Compassionate.

—'Abdu'l-Bahá

I have wakened in Thy shelter,
O my God, and it becometh him that
seeketh that shelter to abide within
the Sanctuary of Thy protection
and the Stronghold of Thy defense.
Illumine my inner being, O my Lord,
with the splendors of the Dayspring
of Thy Revelation, even as thou didst
illumine my outer being with the
morning light of Thy favor.

—Bahá'u'lláh

I have risen this morning by Thy
grace, O my God, and left my
home trusting wholly in Thee, and
committing myself to Thy care.
Send down, then, upon me, out of
the heaven of Thy mercy, a blessing
from Thy side, and enable me to
return home in safety even as Thou
didst enable me to set out under Thy
protection with my thoughts fixed
steadfastly upon Thee.

There is none other God but Thee,
the One, the Incomparable,
the All-Knowing, the All-Wise.

—Bahá'u'lláh

When you wake up
in the morning

O my God, my Master, the Goal of my desire! This, Thy servant, seeketh to sleep in the shelter of Thy mercy, and to repose beneath the canopy of Thy grace, imploring Thy care and Thy protection.

I beg of Thee, O my Lord, by Thine eye that sleepeth not, to guard mine eyes from beholding aught beside Thee. Strengthen, then, their vision that they may discern Thy signs, and behold the Horizon of Thy Revelation. Thou art He before the revelations of Whose omnipotence the quintessence of power hath trembled. No God is there but Thee, the Almighty, the All-Subduing, the Unconditioned.

—Bahá'u'lláh

O seeker of Truth! If thou desirest that God may open thine eye, thou must supplicate unto God, pray to and commune with Him at midnight, saying:

O Lord, I have turned my face unto Thy kingdom of oneness and am immersed in the sea of Thy mercy. O Lord, enlighten my sight by beholding Thy lights in this dark night, and make me happy by the wine of Thy love in this wonderful age. O Lord, make me hear Thy call, and open before my face the doors of Thy heaven, so that I may see the light of Thy glory and become attracted to Thy beauty.

Verily, Thou art the Giver, the Generous, the Merciful, the Forgiving.

—'Abdu'l-Bahá

Before going to sleep

www.ingramcontent.com/pod-product-compliance
Lightning Source LLC
Chambersburg PA
CBHW040246150626
46547CB00041B/2994